30180

WELCOME TO THE U.S.A.

ALASKA

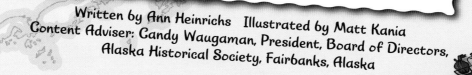

Written by Ann Heinrichs   Illustrated by Matt Kania
Content Adviser: Candy Waugaman, President, Board of Directors,
Alaska Historical Society, Fairbanks, Alaska

The Child's World

Published in the United States of America by The Child's World®
PO Box 326 • Chanhassen, MN 55317-0326
800-599-READ • www.childsworld.com

Photo Credits
Cover: Getty Images/Photographer's Choice/Johnny Johnson;
frontispiece: Photodisc.

Interior: Alaska Day Festival: 13; Alaska Division of Tourism: 9, 14 (R. Valentine), 17 (Mike Affleck), 18 (June Mackie/FCVB), 25, 26 (Robert Angell), 29 (Mark Wayne), 38; Alaska State Library – Historical Collections: 20; Corbis: 10 (James Marshall), 22 (Jim Sugar), 30 (Paul A. Souders), 33 (David Samuel Robbins); Getty Images: 21 (Hulton|Archive), 34 (Allsport/Ezra O. Shaw); Library of Congress: 12; Clark James Mishler/Alaska Native Heritage Center: 6.

Acknowledgments
The Child's World®: Mary Berendes, Publishing Director

Editorial Directions, Inc.: E. Russell Primm, Editorial Director; Katie Marsico, Associate Editor; Judith Shiffer, Assistant Editor; Matt Messbarger, Editorial Assistant; Susan Hindman, Copy Editor; Melissa McDaniel, Proofreader; Peter Garnham, Matt Messbarger, Olivia Nellums, Chris Simms, Molly Symmonds, Katherine Trickle, Carl Stephen Wender, Fact Checkers; Tim Griffin/IndexServ, Indexer; Cian Loughlin O'Day, Photo Researcher and Editor

The Design Lab: Kathleen Petelinsek, Design and art production

Library of Congress Cataloging-in-Publication Data
Heinrichs, Ann.
  Alaska / written by Ann Heinrichs ; cartography and illustrations by Matt Kania.
    p. cm. — (Welcome to the U.S.A.)
  Includes index.
  ISBN 1-59296-371-4 (library bound : alk. paper) 1. Alaska—Juvenile literature.
I. Kania, Matt. II. Title. III. Series.
  F904.3.H448 2006
  979.8—dc22   2004026161

Ann Heinrichs is the author of more than 100 books for children and young adults. She has also enjoyed successful careers as a children's book editor and an advertising copywriter. Ann grew up in Fort Smith, Arkansas, and lives in Chicago, Illinois.

About the Author
Ann Heinrichs

Matt Kania loves maps and, as a kid, dreamed of making them. In school he studied geography and cartography, and today he makes maps for a living. Matt's favorite thing about drawing maps is learning about the places they represent. Many of the maps he has created can be found in books, magazines, videos, Web sites, and public places.

About the
Map Illustrator
Matt Kania

On the cover: Watch out—hungry polar bears call Alaska home!
On page one: Visitors enjoy a scenic cruise in Glacier Bay.

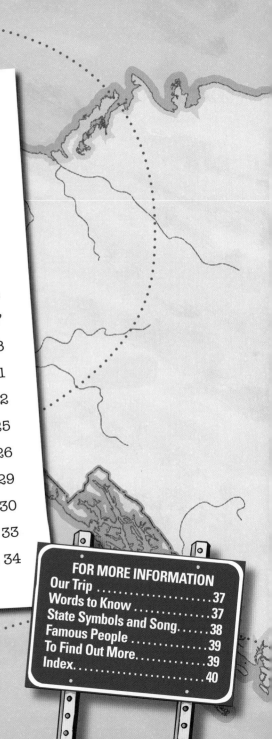

OUR ALASKA TRIP

Alaska's Nicknames: The Last Frontier and Land of the Midnight Sun

Ready to explore the Last **Frontier**? Just hop aboard. We're heading north to Alaska! You'll meet sled dogs and polar bears. You'll see the Sun shine at midnight. You'll climb glaciers and stroll among totem poles. You'll fish for halibut and pan for gold. Can you dig it? Then buckle up and hang on tight. We're off!

WELCOME TO ALASKA

As you travel through Alaska, watch for all the interesting facts along the way.

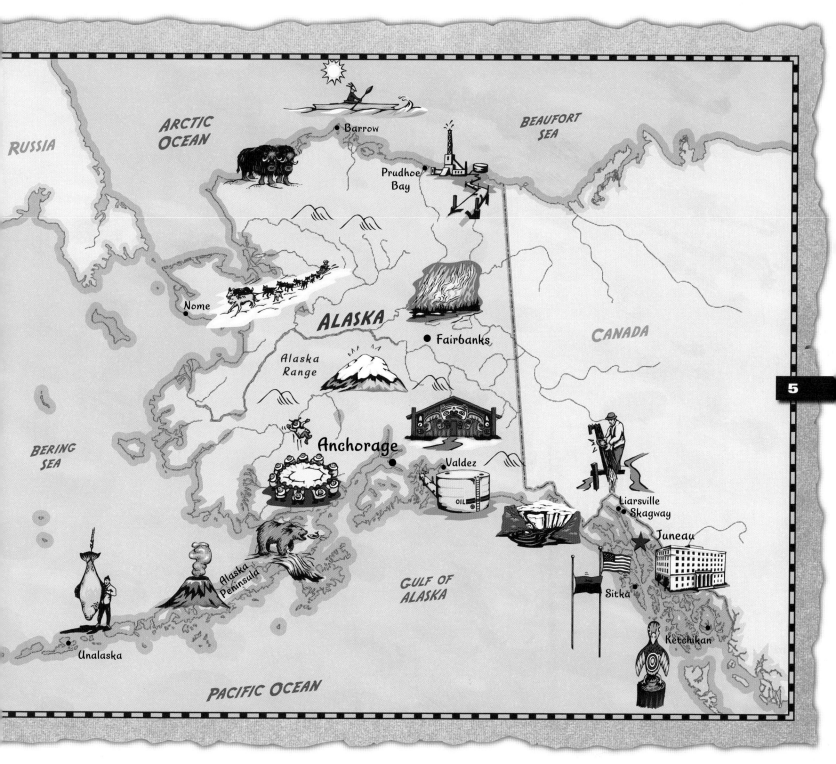

RUSSIA

ARCTIC OCEAN

BEAUFORT SEA

• Barrow

Prudhoe Bay

Nome •

ALASKA

• Fairbanks

CANADA

Alaska Range

Anchorage

Valdez

Liarsville
Skagway

Juneau

BERING SEA

OIL

Sitka

Alaska Peninsula

GULF OF ALASKA

Ketchikan

Unalaska

PACIFIC OCEAN

Wow! They've got 5 Native villages with Alaska Natives explaining stuff!

You're hearing ancient stories. You're holding tools made of moose **antlers.** People are dancing in beaded hides. You're at the Alaska Native Heritage Center!

Here you'll learn all about Alaska's Natives. They began living in Alaska thousands of years ago. They hunted and fished. They made their own clothes, tools, and houses. Some made homes with whale bones. Some made lamps that burned seal oil. Everyone took what they needed from their surroundings.

6

Want to learn more about Alaska Natives? Be sure to visit Alaska Native Heritage Center!

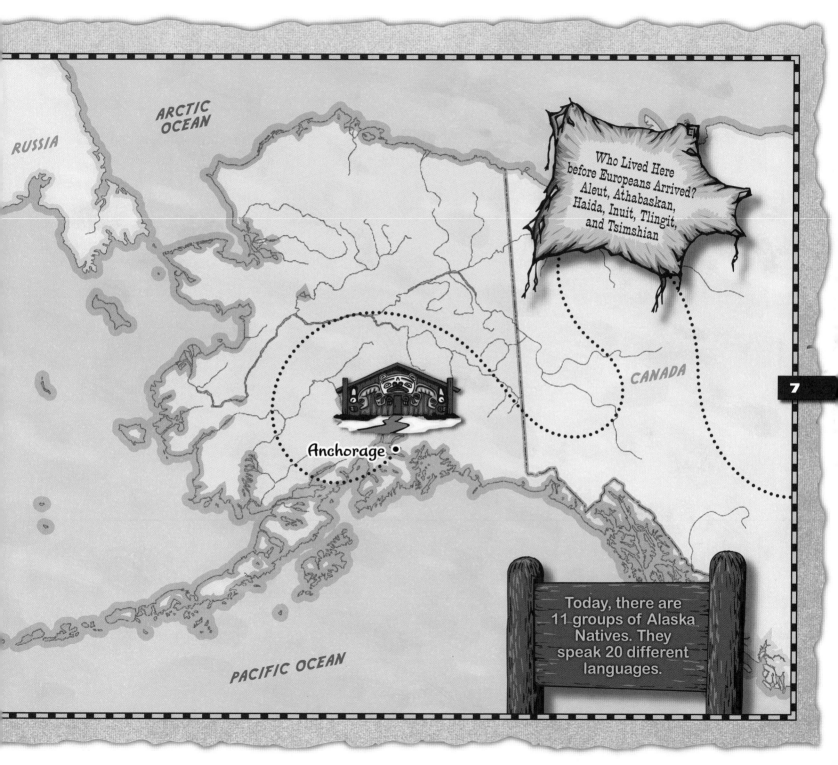

ARCTIC OCEAN

RUSSIA

Who Lived Here before Europeans Arrived? Aleut, Athabaskan, Haida, Inuit, Tlingit, and Tsimshian

CANADA

Anchorage

PACIFIC OCEAN

Today, there are 11 groups of Alaska Natives. They speak 20 different languages.

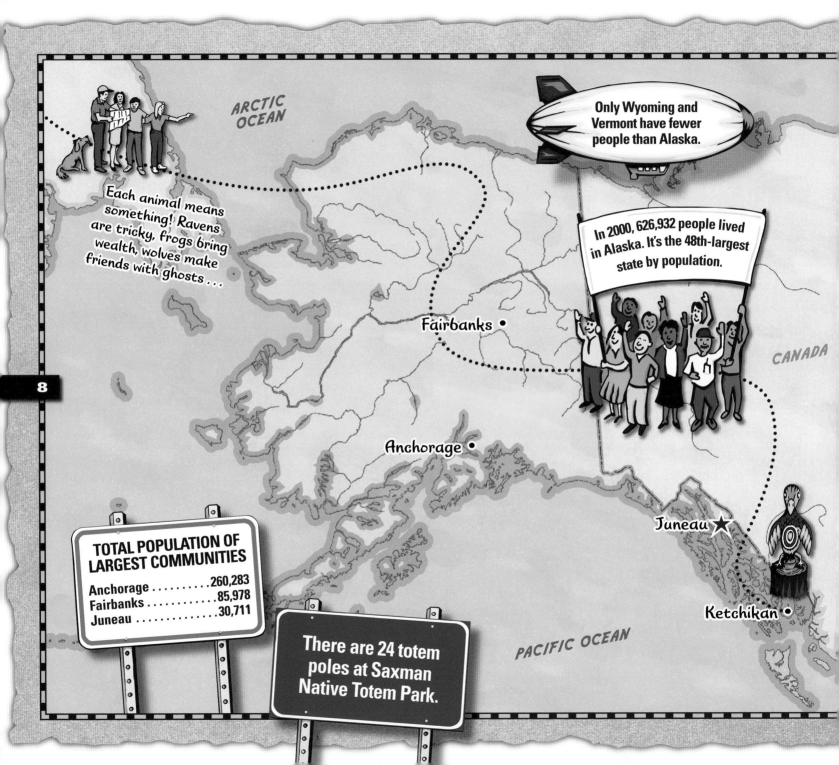

ARCTIC OCEAN

Only Wyoming and Vermont have fewer people than Alaska.

Each animal means something! Ravens are tricky, frogs bring wealth, wolves make friends with ghosts ...

In 2000, 626,932 people lived in Alaska. It's the 48th-largest state by population.

Fairbanks •

CANADA

Anchorage •

Juneau ★

TOTAL POPULATION OF LARGEST COMMUNITIES

Anchorage 260,283
Fairbanks 85,978
Juneau 30,711

Ketchikan •

There are 24 totem poles at Saxman Native Totem Park.

PACIFIC OCEAN

Saxman Native Totem Park

Yo! Look up! There's a wolf. There's an eagle. There's a **thunderbird** with gigantic wings!

You're strolling through Saxman Native Totem Park near Ketchikan. Those animals are carved on totem poles. Alaska's Tlingit and Haida people carve these poles. The poles tell **legends** and family histories.

About one in six Alaskans is a Native. Many still hunt and fish for a living. They also carry on their arts and customs. Most non-Natives live around the big cities.

Some Alaskans live out in the wilderness. No roads reach their homes. Much of Alaska is still unsettled. That's why it's called the Last Frontier.

Totem poles are like storybooks. This carving is part of the story.

Let's go! They've got snowshoe softball, ice bowling, and sled dog races!

The Anchorage Fur Rendezvous celebrates winter's end. The fun and games last 10 whole days!

10

Is she flying? Is she falling from the sky? Well, yes and no. It's the Anchorage Fur **Rendezvous.** And you're watching the blanket toss!

Eskimos celebrated whale hunts with a blanket toss. They held the edges of a big blanket. Then they tossed someone up in the air. It was just like a trampoline!

Russians were the first non-Natives in Alaska. They were explorers and fur traders. Traders and Natives would meet at a rendezvous. They shared food, customs, and news. And they played games such as the blanket toss!

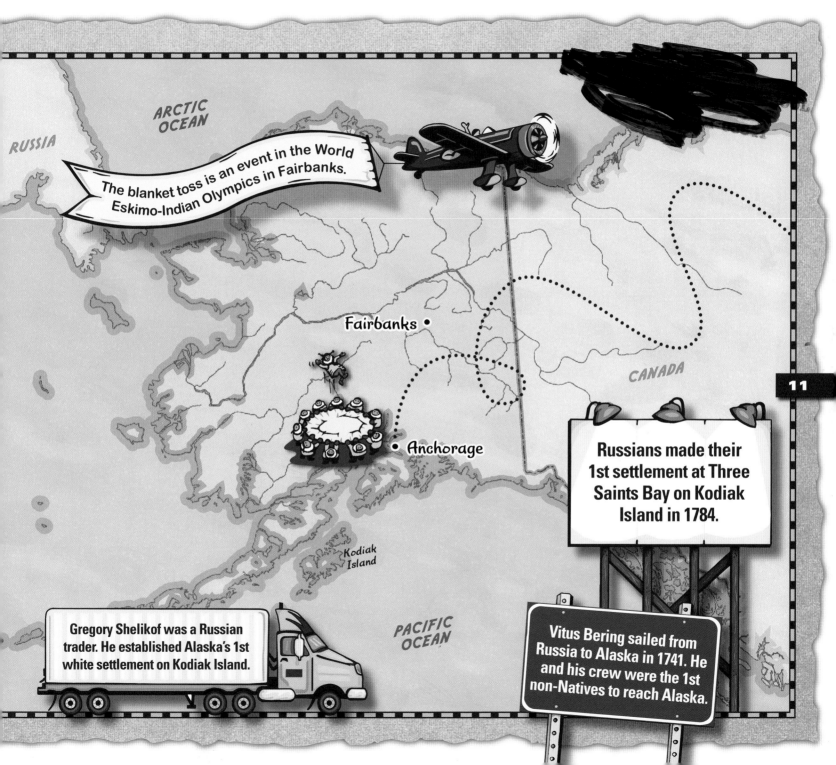

ARCTIC OCEAN

RUSSIA

The blanket toss is an event in the World Eskimo-Indian Olympics in Fairbanks.

Fairbanks •

CANADA

• Anchorage

Russians made their 1st settlement at Three Saints Bay on Kodiak Island in 1784.

Kodiak Island

PACIFIC OCEAN

Gregory Shelikof was a Russian trader. He established Alaska's 1st white settlement on Kodiak Island.

Vitus Bering sailed from Russia to Alaska in 1741. He and his crew were the 1st non-Natives to reach Alaska.

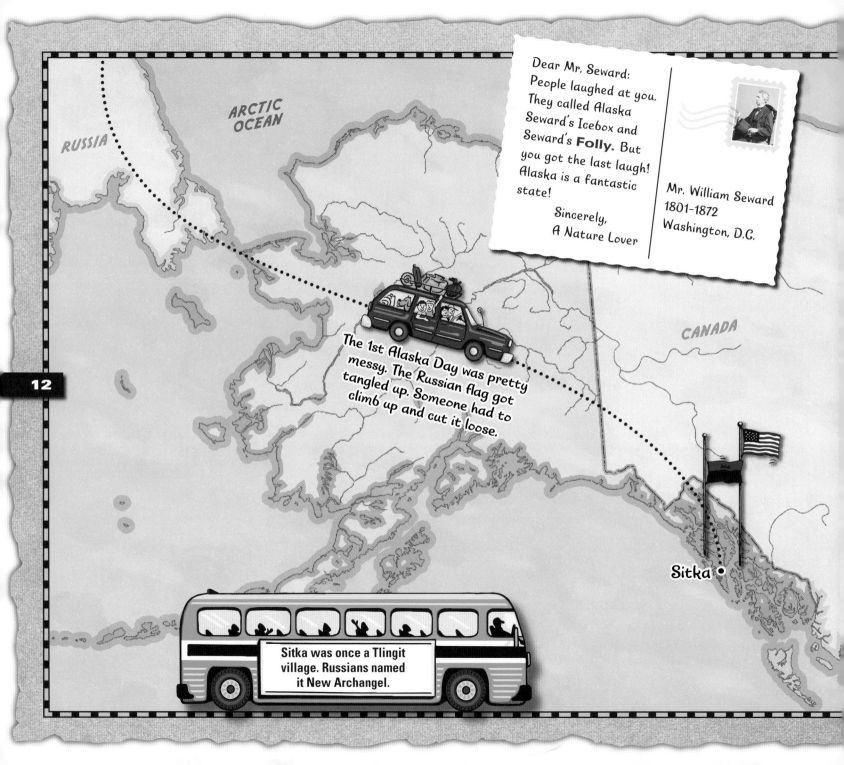

ARCTIC OCEAN

RUSSIA

CANADA

Dear Mr. Seward:
People laughed at you.
They called Alaska
Seward's Icebox and
Seward's **Folly.** But
you got the last laugh!
Alaska is a fantastic
state!

Sincerely,
A Nature Lover

Mr. William Seward
1801–1872
Washington, D.C.

The 1st Alaska Day was pretty messy. The Russian flag got tangled up. Someone had to climb up and cut it loose.

Sitka

Sitka was once a Tlingit village. Russians named it New Archangel.

Alaska Day in Sitka

Down comes the Russian flag. Up goes the American flag. It's Alaska Day in Sitka!

This festival celebrates a big day for Alaska. It was October 18, 1867. The place was Sitka, Alaska's Russian capital. That day, Russia transferred Alaska to the United States. People act out the ceremony every year. It happens on Sitka's Castle Hill.

William Seward was the U.S. secretary of state. He wanted to buy Alaska. People thought he was crazy. But Seward knew Alaska was a rich land. It had lots of fish, lumber, and minerals. How much did the United States pay for Alaska? More than $7 million!

Is it 1867? No, it's just a reenactment on Sitka's Castle Hill.

Saint Michael's Cathedral in Sitka is a beautiful Russian Orthodox church.

14

Smoosh. Squish. Squoosh. What's that under your feet? It's Arctic **tundra**! Northern Alaska is the Arctic Region. It faces the Arctic Ocean. Its icy soil is called tundra. This soil is frozen just beneath the surface. Walk on tundra and it feels spongy!

Alaska is a big **peninsula.** Water surrounds almost all of it. Alaska has two long "tails." One is on the southeast. It's called the Panhandle. The other is on the southwest. It's the Alaska Peninsula and the Aleutian Islands.

Alaska has two big mountain ranges. The Brooks Range is in the north. In central Alaska is the Alaska Range. Alaska also has lots of glaciers. They look like mountains of ice.

Dall sheep are common on the Brooks Range. Moose, wolves, and brown bears live there, too.

Forty-eight U.S. states are connected to each other. Alaskans call them the Lower 48.

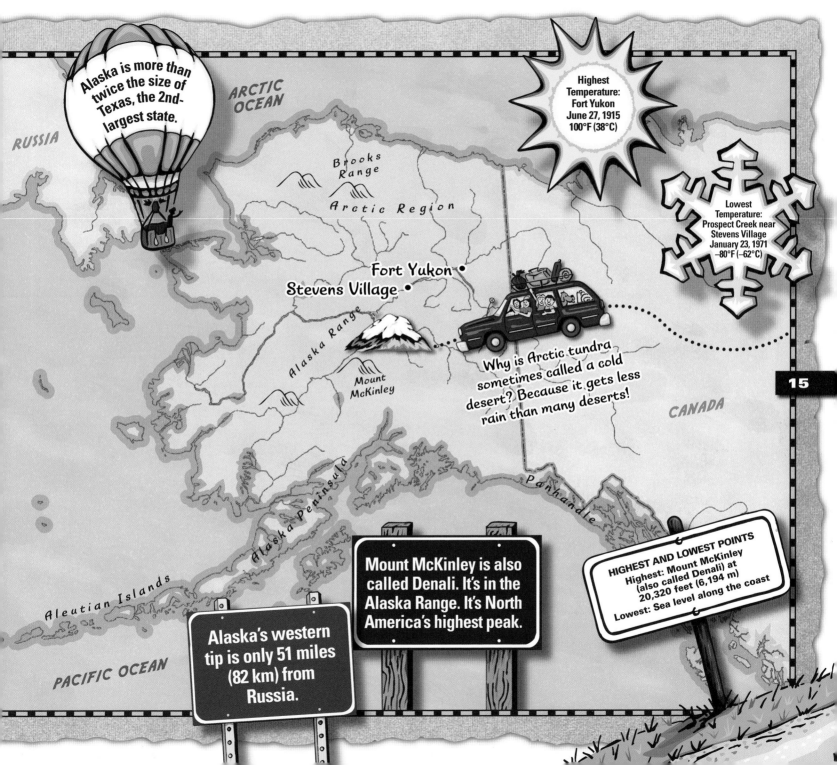

Alaska is more than twice the size of Texas, the 2nd-largest state.

ARCTIC OCEAN

RUSSIA

Highest Temperature: Fort Yukon June 27, 1915 100°F (38°C)

Brooks Range

Arctic Region

Lowest Temperature: Prospect Creek near Stevens Village January 23, 1971 −80°F (−62°C)

Fort Yukon •
Stevens Village •

Alaska Range

Mount McKinley

Why is Arctic tundra sometimes called a cold desert? Because it gets less rain than many deserts!

CANADA

15

Panhandle

Alaska Peninsula

Aleutian Islands

Mount McKinley is also called Denali. It's in the Alaska Range. It's North America's highest peak.

HIGHEST AND LOWEST POINTS
Highest: Mount McKinley (also called Denali) at 20,320 feet (6,194 m)
Lowest: Sea level along the coast

Alaska's western tip is only 51 miles (82 km) from Russia.

PACIFIC OCEAN

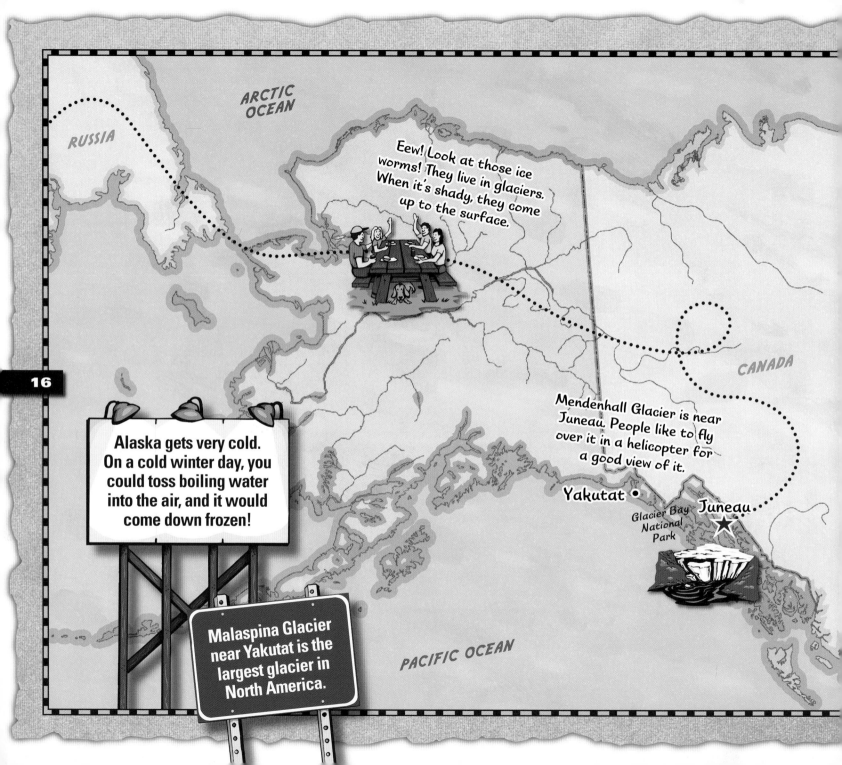

You set your backpack down. You went off and had lunch. Now you're back, but the backpack is somewhere else. So who moved that backpack?

Nobody did! You're in Glacier Bay National Park. You set your backpack by a glacier. The glacier looks like an ice mountain. But it's really a river of ice. It moves!

Glacier Bay is near Juneau. Its glaciers are awesome! Sometimes a big chunk of ice breaks off. That's called calving. Why? Because it's like a cow having a calf!

There's lots to do in Glacier Bay. Go camping, rafting, or even take a cruise!

The northern lights are one of nature's wonders.
They're an awesome sight to behold.

Watching the Northern Lights

Go to Fairbanks, and wait for night to fall. You're in for a fantastic show! The northern lights are flashing across the sky. They're like dancing curtains of color! People come from miles away to see them.

There's a lot to do outdoors in Alaska. Some people like to watch the northern lights. Others climb mountains, ride kayaks, or fish. Denali National Park is popular, too. Some people cruise the Inside Passage. That's a waterway along the Panhandle.

It's hard to get around in Alaska. Many people travel in bush planes. Some ride dogsleds or snowmobiles! The Marine Highway runs along the southeast coast. It's just for boats. These boats are like water taxis!

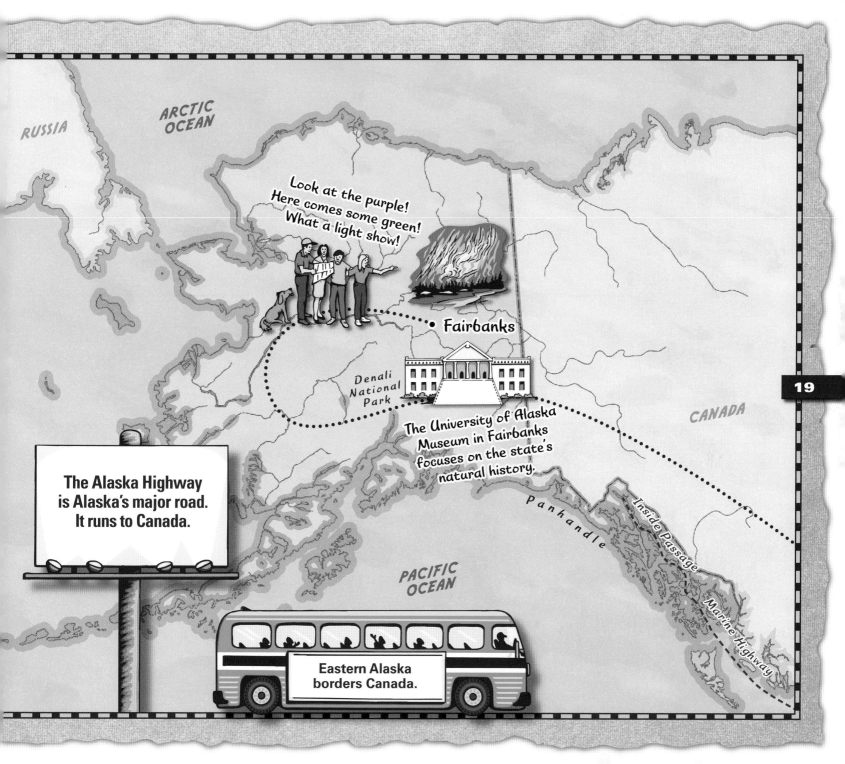

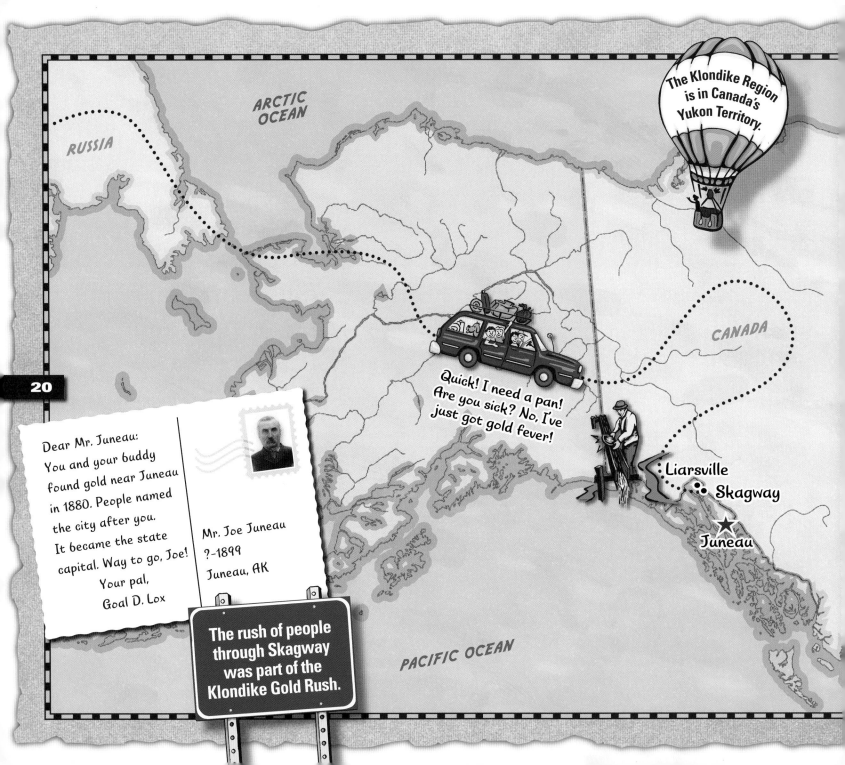

Liarsville and the Klondike Gold Rush

There's a speck! There's a fleck! It's gold! You're panning for gold in Liarsville. It's just outside of Skagway.

Thousands of people swarmed into Skagway in 1897. They'd heard about gold in Canada's Klondike Region. People got their gold-mining supplies in Skagway.

Liarsville stands where a gold-miner's camp used to be. According to legend, reporters camped there, too. They were looking for exciting stories to write. But they didn't want to hike to the Klondike. So they made up stories about big gold finds!

Gold hunters eagerly traveled to the Klondike Region. They hoped to make their fortunes there.

The Prudhoe Bay Oil Field

Days on the oil field are long and cold. But the pay is quite good!

The workers have to watch out for bears when they're working outside!

They work twelve hours a day. They sleep in **dorms.** Is this some kind of labor camp? Yes! It's a workers' camp at Prudhoe Bay.

Oil was discovered at Prudhoe Bay in 1968. It's way up on the north coast. Suddenly, oil became Alaska's richest product.

The oil at Prudhoe Bay is trapped underground. Workers drill down to reach it. Almost 2,000 people work at Prudhoe Bay. They work seven days a week. Then they get a week off. What a life!

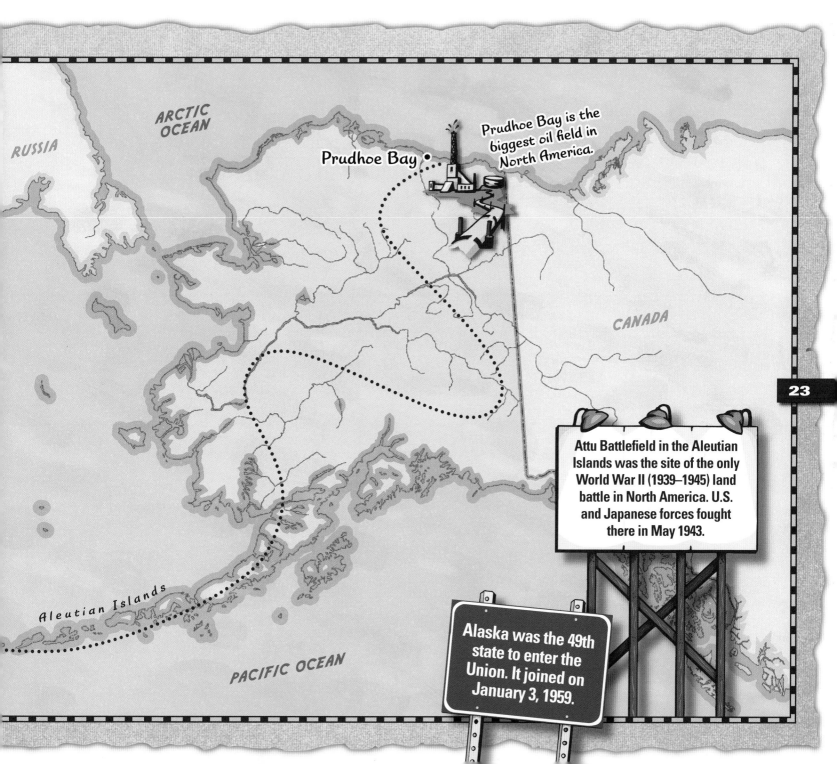

ARCTIC OCEAN

RUSSIA

Prudhoe Bay •

Prudhoe Bay is the biggest oil field in North America.

CANADA

Attu Battlefield in the Aleutian Islands was the site of the only World War II (1939–1945) land battle in North America. U.S. and Japanese forces fought there in May 1943.

Aleutian Islands

PACIFIC OCEAN

Alaska was the 49th state to enter the Union. It joined on January 3, 1959.

The Trans-Alaska Pipeline

Holy moley! It's silvery and shiny. It's long and round and fat. And it's zigzagging across the tundra. Is it a monster snake? No, silly! It's just the Trans-Alaska Pipeline.

Oil mining is Alaska's biggest **industry.** Oil is the most valuable mining product, too. Most of the oil comes from Prudhoe Bay. The oil travels through that huge pipeline. It goes to the port of Valdez. That's in south-central Alaska. Look at that pipeline from the air. It looks like a big silver snake!

The Trans-Alaska Pipeline is hundreds of miles long. Billions of barrels of oil have moved through it.

An instrument called a pig is in the pipeline. It has a computer to make sure nothing is blocking the oil flow.

Katmai and Its Fishing Bears

It must be lunchtime! These brown bears are fishing in Katmai National Park.

Alaska has 16 national wildlife refuges. The National Park Service has 18 sites in Alaska.

Swoosh! The bear scoops up a salmon. Chomp! What a great snack! This is no zoo. You're in Katmai National Park on the Alaska Peninsula. More than 2,000 brown bears live there. Their favorite food? Salmon!

Alaska has lots of bears, deer, and moose. Mountain goats and sheep live in the mountains. Polar bears roam along the icy north coast. You'll see seals and seabirds along the coast, too. Look out in the water. You might see whales leaping!

Not much grows on the northern tundra. Mostly there are mosses and short grasses. Caribou graze on these plants. Caribou are a kind of reindeer. Can Santa be far away?

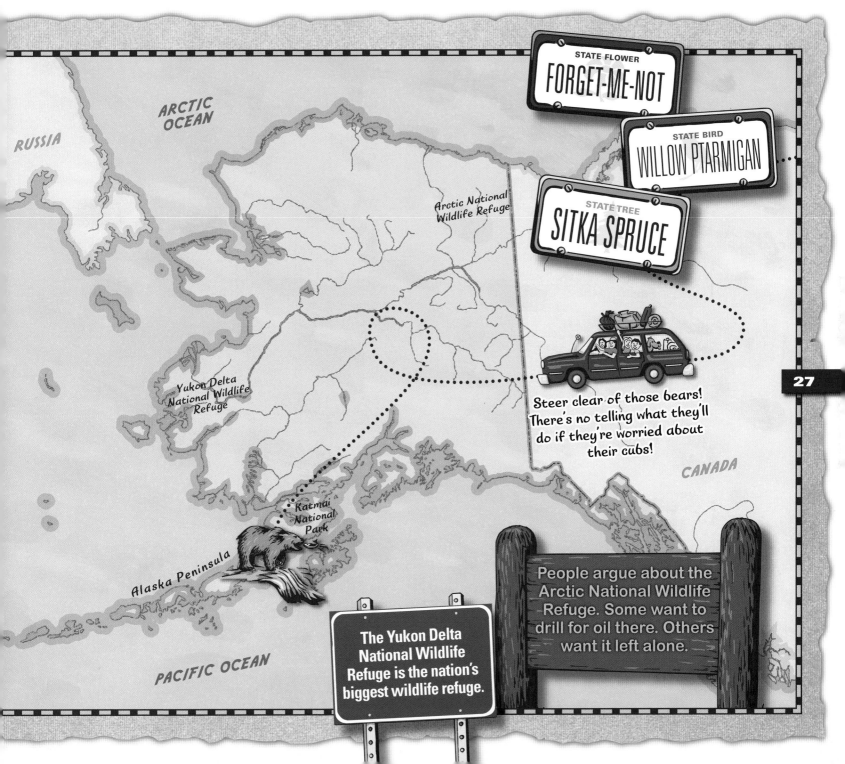

ARCTIC OCEAN

RUSSIA

Arctic National
Wildlife Refuge

STATE FLOWER
FORGET-ME-NOT

STATE BIRD
WILLOW PTARMIGAN

STATE TREE
SITKA SPRUCE

Steer clear of those bears!
There's no telling what they'll
do if they're worried about
their cubs!

CANADA

Yukon Delta
National Wildlife
Refuge

Katmai
National
Park

Alaska Peninsula

PACIFIC OCEAN

The Yukon Delta
National Wildlife
Refuge is the nation's
biggest wildlife refuge.

People argue about the
Arctic National Wildlife
Refuge. Some want to
drill for oil there. Others
want it left alone.

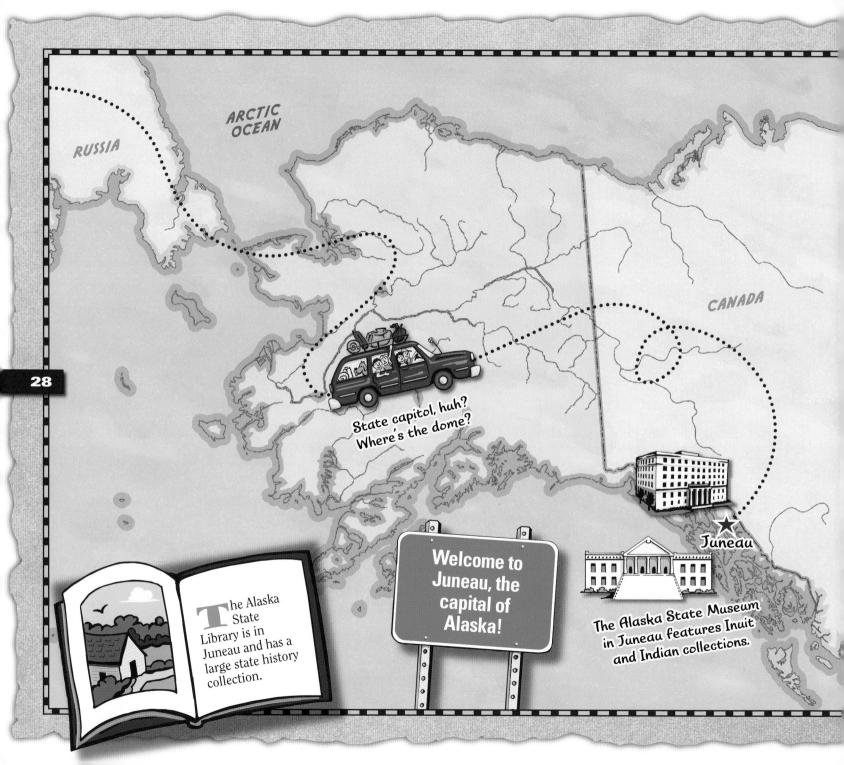

ARCTIC OCEAN

RUSSIA

CANADA

State capitol, huh? Where's the dome?

Juneau

The Alaska State Museum in Juneau features Inuit and Indian collections.

Welcome to Juneau, the capital of Alaska!

The Alaska State Library is in Juneau and has a large state history collection.

Alaska's state motto is North to the Future.

Alaska's state capitol stands in Juneau. Most capitols have a dome, but not Alaska's. It just has a regular flat roof. That's okay. People inside the capitol run the state government. Who needs a dome for that?

Alaska has three branches of government. One branch makes the laws. It's called the legislature. Another branch carries out the laws. The governor heads this branch. The third branch consists of state courts. Their judges decide if laws have been broken.

Alaska's citizens helped raise money to buy the land for the capitol.

29

Kodiak is an important fishing port. It ranks among the top 3 U.S. ports.

Jack Tragis caught a huge halibut near Unalaska in 1996. It weighed 459 pounds (208 kg)! That became the world record.

Unalaska's World Record Halibut Derby

That is one big fish. But is it big enough? If it is, you get $100,000! You're at the Unalaska World Record Halibut Derby. Just catch the biggest halibut ever. Then you win the prize!

Alaska has the nation's biggest fishing industry. Unalaska is an important fishing port. It's in the Aleutian Islands. Kodiak is another important port. Crab, scallop, and shrimp are important catches. So are cod, flounder, and salmon. And don't forget that halibut!

Farming is a small industry in Alaska. The growing season is not very long. The short summer gets lots of sunshine, though. Some farming areas get twenty sunny hours a day!

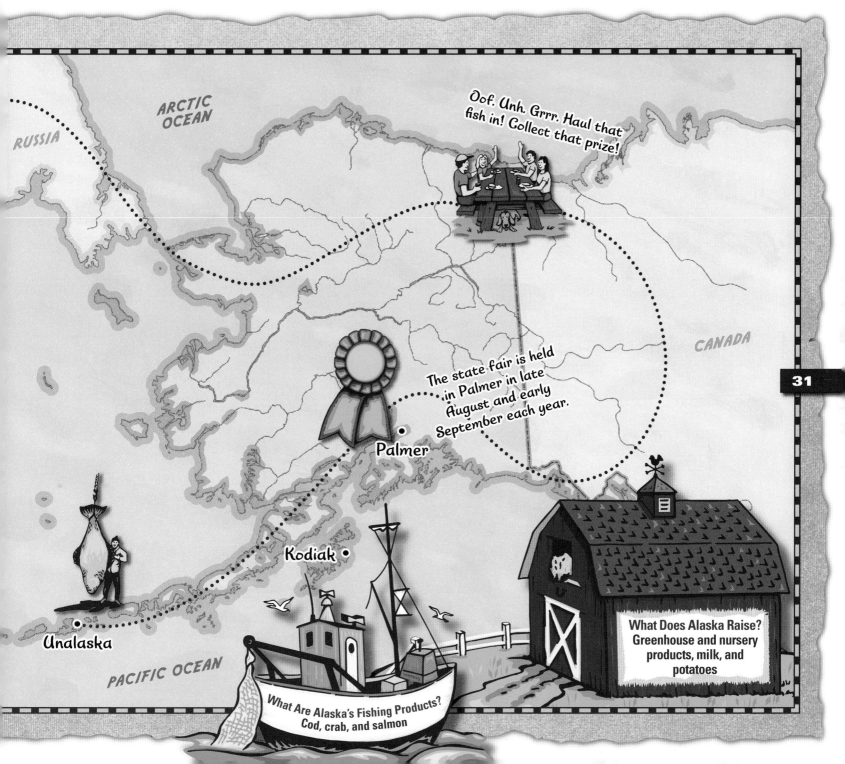

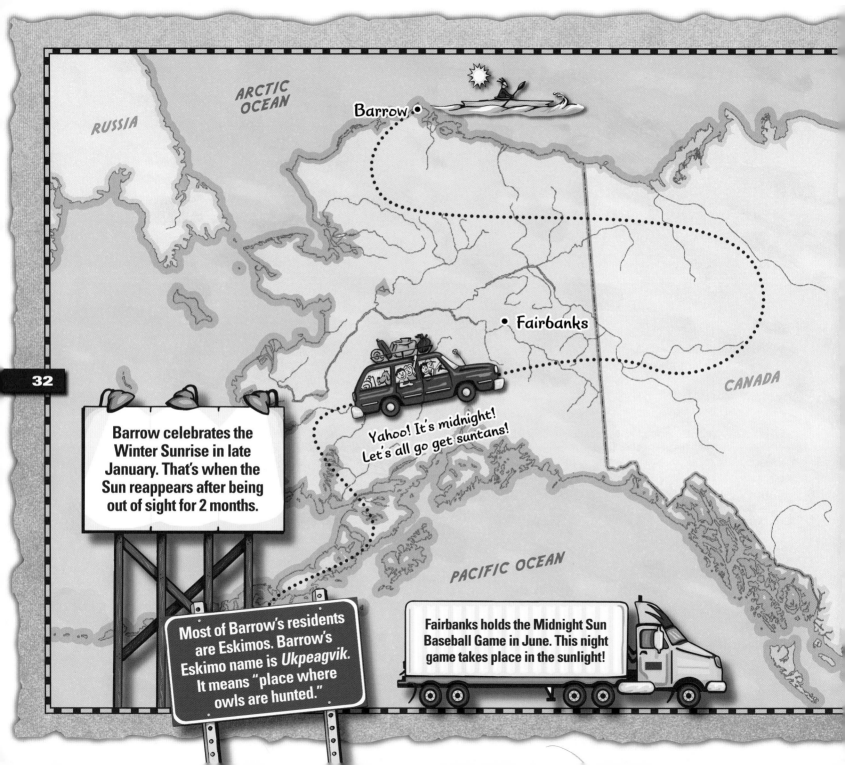

ARCTIC OCEAN

RUSSIA

Barrow

Fairbanks

CANADA

PACIFIC OCEAN

Yahoo! It's midnight!
Let's all go get suntans!

Barrow celebrates the Winter Sunrise in late January. That's when the Sun reappears after being out of sight for 2 months.

Most of Barrow's residents are Eskimos. Barrow's Eskimo name is *Ukpeagvik*. It means "place where owls are hunted."

Fairbanks holds the Midnight Sun Baseball Game in June. This night game takes place in the sunlight!

Barrow and the Midnight Sun

Your watch says twelve o'clock. The Sun is shining. So it must be noon, right? Wrong! It's midnight! You're in Barrow during the Midnight Sun!

Barrow is Alaska's most northerly city. Its summers are really sunny. The Sun doesn't set for almost three months! It's the opposite in winter. For two whole months, the Sun never rises!

How does the Midnight Sun happen? Like this. The Earth is tilted as it turns around. In the summer, the far north tilts toward the Sun. That's why it gets more hours of sunshine. In the winter, the north is tilted the other way. It tilts away from the Sun. Then the north gets more hours of darkness.

It never gets dark during Barrow's summers? Cool—I can ride my bike at midnight!

Mush, you huskies! Mush!

Nome and the Iditarod

34

The dogs dash to the finish line. Their tongues are hanging out. They've been racing for days and days. For those dogs, there's no place like Nome!

Nome is where the Iditarod ends. That's a sled dog race. The sled drivers are called mushers. Their dogs are huskies. They race over mountains, forests, and frozen rivers. They race through darkness, wind, and cold. At last, they can rest and eat some treats. Good doggies!

C'mon, we're almost to the finish line! Racing in the Iditarod requires skill and speed.

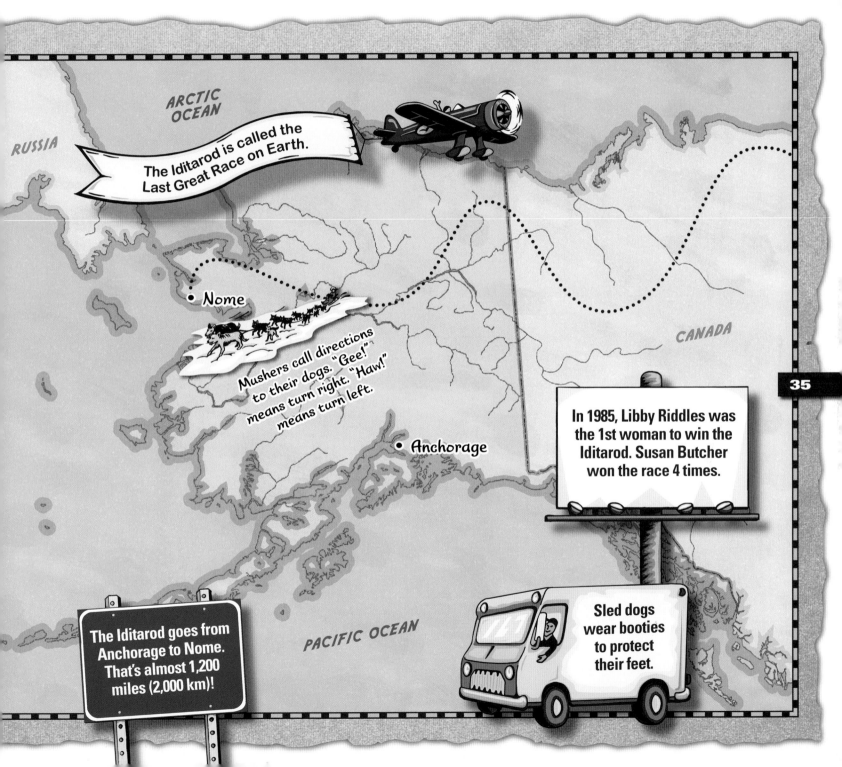

ARCTIC OCEAN

RUSSIA

The Iditarod is called the Last Great Race on Earth.

Nome

Mushers call directions to their dogs. "Gee!" means turn right. "Haw!" means turn left.

CANADA

In 1985, Libby Riddles was the 1st woman to win the Iditarod. Susan Butcher won the race 4 times.

Anchorage

The Iditarod goes from Anchorage to Nome. That's almost 1,200 miles (2,000 km)!

PACIFIC OCEAN

Sled dogs wear booties to protect their feet.

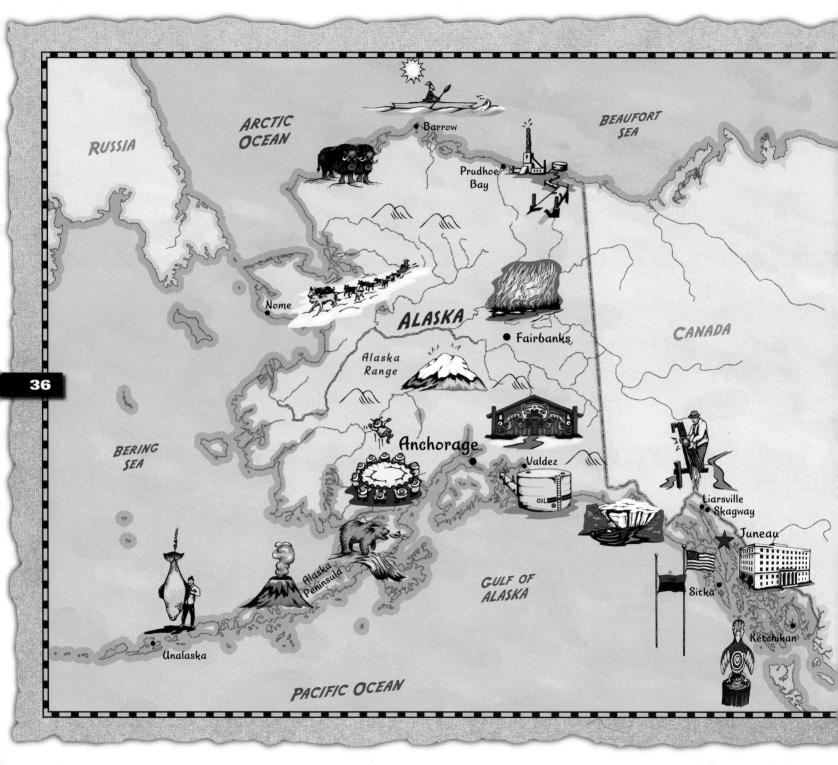

OUR TRIP

We visited many amazing places on our trip! We also met a lot of interesting people along the way. Look at the map on the left. Use your finger to trace all the places we have been.

What states have fewer people than Alaska? See page 8 for the answer.

What is the other name for Mount McKinley? Page 15 has the answer.

What is the largest glacier in North America? See page 16 for the answer.

What happened at Attu Battlefield? Look on page 23 for the answer.

What is the nation's biggest wildlife refuge? Page 27 has the answer.

What city is the state capital? Turn to page 28 for the answer.

How big was Jack Tragis's halibut? Look on page 30 and find out!

How many miles does the Iditarod cover? Turn to page 35 for the answer.

That was a great trip! We have traveled all over Alaska!
  There are a few places that we didn't have time for, though. Next time, we plan to visit the Valley of Ten Thousand Smokes. It's located along the Alaska Peninsula. There are 15 active volcanoes there!

More Places to Visit in Alaska

WORDS TO KNOW

antlers (ANT-lurz) bony structures like horns on the heads of deer and related animals

dorms (DORMZ) short for dormitories; buildings where a lot of people sleep

folly (FOL-ee) something foolish

frontier (fruhn-TIHR) an unexplored region

industry (IN-duh-stree) a type of business

legends (LEJ-uhndz) imaginary tales that people tell to explain their world

peninsula (puh-NIN-suh-luh) a piece of land almost completely surrounded by water

rendezvous (RON-day-voo) French word for a meeting

thunderbird (THUHN-dur-burd) to Alaska Natives, a huge, imaginary bird with magical powers

tundra (TUHN-druh) soil that's frozen beneath the surface all year round

Alaska covers 571,951 square miles (1,481,347 sq km). It's the largest state in size.

STATE SYMBOLS

State bird: Willow ptarmigan

State fish: King salmon

State flower: Forget-me-not

State fossil: Woolly mammoth

State gem: Jade

State insect: Four-spotted skimmer dragonfly

State land mammal: Moose

State marine mammal: Bowhead whale

State mineral: Gold

State sport: Dog mushing

State tree: Sitka spruce

State flag

State seal

STATE SONG

"Alaska's Flag"

Words by Marie Drake, music by Elinor Dusenbury

Eight stars of gold on a field of blue—
Alaska's flag. May it mean to you
The blue of the sea, the evening sky,
The mountain lakes, and the flow'rs nearby,
The gold of the early sourdough's dreams,
The precious gold of the hills and streams;
The brilliant stars in the northern sky,
The *Bear*—the *Dipper*—and, shining high,
The great North Star with its steady light,
Over land and sea a beacon bright.
Alaska's flag—to Alaskans dear,
The simple flag of a last frontier.

FAMOUS PEOPLE

Baranov, Aleksandr (1746–1819), Russian fur trader, politician

Bering, Vitus (1680–1741), explorer

Boozer, Carlos (1981–), basketball player

Brooks, Alfred Hulse (1871–1924), geologist

Egan, William (1914–1984), 1st elected governor

Eielson, Carl (1897–1929), pioneer pilot

Jackson, Sheldon (1834–1909), missionary and educator

London, Jack (1876–1916), author

Fletcher, Rosey (1975–), snowboarder

Gaines, Ruben (1912–1994), poet

George, Jean Craighead (1919–), children's author

Gomez, Scott (1979–), hockey player

Jewel (1974–), singer, songwriter

Mala, Ray (1906–1952), actor

Muir, John (1838–1914), naturalist

Murkowski, Frank (1933–), governor of Alaska

Partch, Virgil F. (1916–1984), cartoonist

Riddles, Libby (1956–), champion musher

Rock, Howard (1911–1976), editor and publisher, activist against nuclear testing

Tosi, Mao (1976–), football player

TO FIND OUT MORE

At the Library
Carne, Carol, and Michael Glenn Monroe (illustrator). *L Is for Last Frontier: An Alaska Alphabet*. Chelsea, Mich.: Sleeping Bear Press, 2002.

Chamberlin-Calamar, Pat, and Shannon Cartwright (illustrator). *Alaska's Twelve Days of Summer*. Seattle: Sasquatch Books, 2003.

Dwyer, Mindy. *The Salmon Princess: An Alaska Cinderella Story*. Seattle: Sasquatch Books, 2004.

Somervill, Barbara A. *Alaska*. New York: Children's Press, 2002.

On the Web
Visit our home page for lots of links about Alaska:
http://www.childsworld.com/links

Note to Parents, Teachers, and Librarians: We routinely verify our Web links to make sure they are safe, active sites—so encourage your readers to check them out!

Places to Visit or Contact
Alaska Travel Industry Association
2600 Cordova Street, Suite 201
Anchorage, AK 99503
907/929-2200
For more information about traveling in Alaska

Anchorage Museum of History & Art
121 W. 7th Avenue
Anchorage, AK 99501
907/343-6173
For more information about the history of Alaska

INDEX

*Bye, Land of the Midnight Sun.
We had a great time.
We'll come back soon!*